Fireflies, Fireflies, Light My Way

By Jonathan London
Illustrated by Linda Messier

Harcourt
SCHOOL PUBLISHERS

Visit The Learning Site!
www.harcourtschool.com

Author's note

"Fireflies, fireflies, light my way" is a line from an old Mesaquakie lullaby, and was the inspiration for this book. The Mesaquakies, otherwise known as the People of the Red Earth, were a large and powerful tribe in the Great Lakes region during the seventeenth and eighteenth centuries. Now they live in a settlement along the Iowa River in Iowa.

It is to the Mesaquakie people that I give thanks for the use of these words.

This edition is published by special arrangement with Viking, A Division of Penguin Young Readers Group, A Member of Penguin Group (USA) Inc.

Grateful acknowledgment is made to Viking Children's Books, A Division of Penguin Young Readers Group, A Member of Penguin Group (USA) Inc. for permission to reprint *Fireflies, Fireflies, Light My Way* by Jonathan London, illustrated by Linda Messier. Text copyright © 1996 by Jonathan London; illustrations copyright © 1996 by Linda Messier.

Printed in China

ISBN 13 978-0-15-351946-8
ISBN 10 0-15-351946-0

2 3 4 5 6 7 8 9 10   985   15 14 13 12 11 10 09 08 07

For Teri, Frank, Jean, Laurie, Marsha, Jane, Melissa, et al.—a writers' group *extraordinaire!*
—J. L.

For Ma and Da
—L. M.

Fireflies, Fireflies, Light My Way

Fireflies, fireflies, light my way.

Lead me to the place . . .

. . . where the turtles play.
Turtles, turtles, dive so deep.

Lead me to the place . . .

. . . where the bullfrogs leap.
Bullfrogs, bullfrogs, leap away.

Lead me to the place . . .

. . . where the beavers play.
Beavers, beavers, gnaw on limbs.

Lead me to the place . . .

. . . where the catfish swims.
Catfish, catfish, swim your best.

Lead me to the place . . .

. . . where the wood ducks nest.
Wood ducks, wood ducks, squawk away.

Lead me to the place . . .

. . . where the muskrats play.
Muskrats, muskrats, paddle far.

Lead me to the place . . .

. . . where the raccoons are.
Raccoons, raccoons, sniff away.

Lead me to the place . . .

. . . where the crawdads stay.
Crawdads, crawdads, scuttle away.

Lead me to the place . . .

. . . where the otters play.
Otters, otters, slide some more.

Lead me to the place . . .

. . . *Yikes!* Where the alligators ROAR?
Alligators, alligators, give me a chance!

Chase me to the place . . .

. . . where the fireflies dance.
Fireflies, fireflies, light my way.

Lead me to the place . . .

. . . where the turtles dive
bullfrogs leap
beavers gnaw
catfish swim
wood ducks squawk
muskrats paddle
raccoons sniff
crawdads scuttle
otters slide . . .

. . . and no alligators chase me away!

Everybody, everybody, sing HURRAY!